Bengal Tiger
Aakash & Adithya's Amazing Wild Facts For Toddlers
Alwina Kindo
AF489246

Dedicated to

My Husband and Four precious gems Aakash, Adithya, Abishek and Sparsha. You make me so proud. Always be the best you can be.
-Mommy

Picture Credits

pixabay.com

Book Info

This book is aligned with the national curriculum standards of science. This book introduces the tiger to the toddler, its habitat, information about it's eye, ears coat, teeth its weight. It's food and hunting habits.The images, repetition of words and phrases support early readers and help the early readers to understand the text. This book introduces early readers to subject - specific vocabulary words which are defined in the glossary section. Toddlers or some early readers may need some assistance to read some of the words.

This Book Belongs to

____

Name

____

Date

New Words

Bengal	Tiger
Mammal	Camouflage
Weigh	Jungles
Sharpest	Distinctive
Patterns	Solitary
Scratch	Caution
Himalayas	Stalk
Waterhole	Canine

Bengal Tigers are mammals

Bengal Tigers belongs to the cat family

Bengal Tigers weigh 396- 583 lbs

Bengal Tigers night vision is 6 times better than ours

Hearing is the tiger's sharpest sense.

Every tiger has a distinctive pattern of black strips on their orange coat

Their claws are used to grip the prey and also to scratch the trees

The male is called tiger and the
female is called tigress

The babies are called cub

Bengal Tigers live in the Himalayas

Tigers are called jungle ghost because they camouflage with the jungle

Tigers usually have social distancing

Bengal Tigers are solitary cats that kill by caution and surprise attack

Bengal Tigers first stalk their prey

Bengal Tigers then charge at their prey

After which they spring on their prey

At last it kills it's prey

Bengal Tigers can kill a buffalo weighing 1,975 lbs nearly 4 times its own weight

Bengal Tigers chase their prey even in
the water

Bengal Tigers kill they prey with a bite to the throat using their canine teeth

Waterhole is a perfect place to drink water and also perfect to catch their prey off guard.

The Bengal Tiger often walks backward into water to keep a watchful eye on its surrounding.

White tigers are not a seperate species, but the result of genetic mutation.

Bengal Tigers combine great power and powerful muscles for hunting successfully

Someone once said, "The Tiger lies low not from fear, but for aim". Be humble and you'll raise higher.

Hope you enjoyed reading this
book.
Check out my other books

www.ingramcontent.com/pod-product-compliance
Lightning Source LLC
Chambersburg PA
CBHW042014110726
48006CB00004B/1079